# THE Dip

**RECLAIMING THE REALITY IN
RELATIONSHIPS BEYOND FEELINGS**

**The Dip //** Reclaiming the Reality in Relationships Beyond Feelings

Copyright © Eastview Christian Church
ISBN 978-0-9841094-5-6

Published in 2011
by
Eastview Christian Church
1500 North Airport Road
Normal, IL 61761

Printed and bound in the USA

All rights reserved. No part of this publication may be reproduced, stored in a retrieval system, or transmitted in any form by any means, eletronic, mechanical, photocopy, recording, or otherwise, without the prior permission of the publisher except as provided by USA copyright law.

Unless otherwise noted, scripture quotations are from the HOLY BIBLE, NEW INTERNATIONAL VERSION®. Copyright © 1973, 1978, 1984 Biblica. Used by permission of Zondervan. All rights reserved.

*To Jamie*
*Thank you for your constant love, patience, forgiveness, and perseverance for a phenomenal, Christ-centered marriage.*

*To Dad*
*Thank you for your display of selfless love and integrity, which have shaped me into the man I am today.*

*To Dann*
*Thank you for teaching me what a disciplemaker of Jesus truly looks like and the beauty of understanding the humanity and lordship of Jesus.*

## [ ACKNOWLEDGEMENTS ]

Words cannot fully express my gratitude…

Thank you Amy Thomas for all the effort, precision, and heart you put into this book through your hours upon hours of editing.

Thank you Chad Cope for all the creativity, passion, and beauty you put into this book through your endless hours of graphic design and layout.

Thank you J.K. Jones and Jim Probst for taking time out of your already packed schedules to read the initial manuscript and offer helpful suggestions and encouragement.

Thank you Cedric Williams for constantly believing in me and pushing me to write this book; without you, I'm not sure this book would have ever been written.

# Table of Contents

**9** [ INTRODUCTION ]
*Expectations Are Everything*

**13** [ CHAPTER ONE ]
*I Feel the Exact Same Way*

**23** [ CHAPTER TWO ]
*So What Exactly Are We?*

**33** [ CHAPTER THREE ]
*You've Changed*

**51** [ CHAPTER FOUR ]
*We're Rich in Love*

**65** [ CHAPTER FIVE ]
*You Lead, and I'll Follow*

**75** [ EPILOGUE ]
*Living So Others Ask Why*

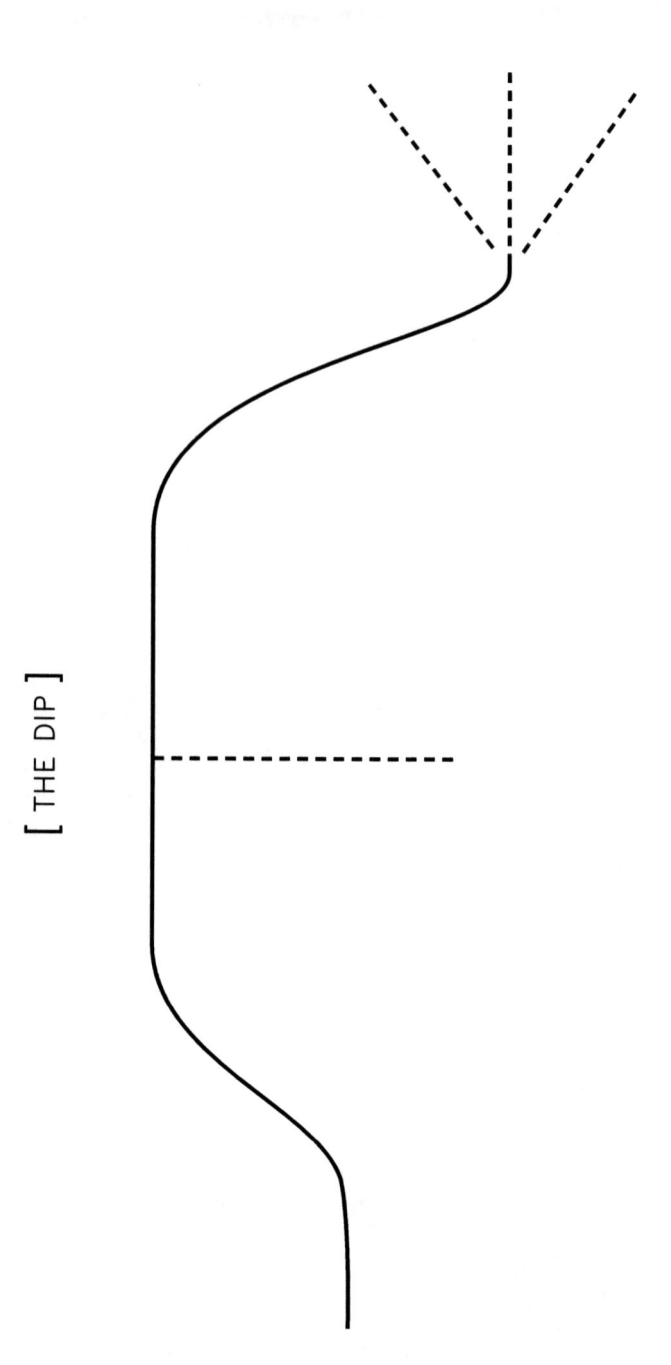

# [ INTRODUCTION ]
# *Expectations Are Everything*

"Expectations are everything."

These three words formed the best piece of advice my wife and I received in our premarital counseling. When we expect something and it happens, we generally feel contentment and satisfaction. However, when we expect something and it doesn't happen, disappointment and frustration are what we're left to sort through.

It's critically important to have realistic expectations.

When two people fall madly in love and decide to get married, it's important that they are encouraged to continue to love each other with that same crazy love all the days of their lives. But it's equally important to be realistic and understand that there will be times along the way that test that love.

Movies today so greatly shape expectations of what being in love looks like. Passion, romance, and sensuality are Hollywood's perfect ingredients for true love. Feelings and emotions dictate everything.

Because of this, most people today want what they see in movies as they look for the perfect someone. Once they find him or her and get married, tt expectations are that feelings will always be strong and intense for one another, that there will be no arguments, and that they will always want to spend every waking moment together.

Now, don't get me wrong—I greatly desire my marriage to be filled with passion, romance, and sensuality. I want my marriage to be phenomenal. I tell couples all the time that they should strive to have an extraordinary marriage and not some run-of-the-mill, mundane, mediocre marriage.

I want my wife and I to someday be that old couple that still holds hands, shares kisses, and can't get enough of each other.

However, while I encourage others to strive for those things, it's important to understand that every moment of marriage isn't puppy love. We can't expect those things each and every moment of each and every day because if we do, we would be constantly let down and disappointed.

Sadly, the divorce rate in our country continues to rise. Nearly half of all first marriages end in divorce, and the rates are even higher for second and third marriages.

*Why is it that so many people get married but don't stay together?*

While I realize there are many contributing factors, I want to focus on one I believe we often ignore. People enter into marriage with unrealistic expectations, and expectations are everything.

Too many people enter into marriage wanting the feeling of love, but not love itself.

Therefore, when feelings begin to fade away, the assumption is that love just faded away, too. It's such a sad reality. If expectations were cast properly in the beginning, maybe more couples would last.

The same is true when considering a relationship with Jesus Christ.

As a pastor, I've watched the same phenomenon that takes place in marriage occur in a person's relationship with Christ: they decide to follow Jesus, but their expectations are unrealistic. The initial surge of emotion becomes an expectation that exists throughout the rest of their journey with Jesus. He or she also believes that since God is now in their life, everything will go their way. Sickness, pain, death, disappointment, and hard times are expected to fall by the wayside because Jesus has made all things new and is on their side.

The problem with these expectations, though, is that they aren't biblical.

Such expectations can't be found in the Scriptures, yet still so many people become Christians with similar unrealistic expectations. Therefore, when troubles befall the new believer, they don't know what to do because it wasn't what was expected.

And just as in a marriage, the result is disillusionment; only this time, in their spiritual walk.

They stop walking.

They divorce Jesus.

Statistics continue to show the constant increase of people walking away from their faith in Christ in today's world, as well as a great number leaving the church. The Barna Group recently released statistics claiming that 18-35 year olds are the least likely to attend a weekly church service, volunteer in a church, participate in a small group, read the Bible, and pray.

Amazingly, they still indicate that their faith is an important part of their lives!

Other experts suggest similar statistics claiming somewhere between 65 and 80 percent of people who grow up in church fall away when they become college-aged. I wholeheartedly believe it's because of unrealistic expectations that are not scripturally based.

This book is about providing realistic expectations as Christ followers and developing perseverance through the inevitable Dip. *The Dip is that point in any and all relationships where feelings begin to fade and commitment has to kick into high gear.* It's that point when you wonder if you're really in love because you don't feel the same way you did when the relationship began.

My absolute favorite person in the Bible (besides Jesus, of course) is the apostle Peter. While most jump on the Paul bandwagon, I'm a huge fan of Peter. I love Peter so much because the books of Matthew, Mark, Luke, John, and the first half of Acts go to great lengths to chronicle his walk with Jesus.

I believe this is because in Peter's life we find a realistic picture of what it looks like to follow Jesus.

Many believe that when they begin following Jesus, everything in their lives will become amazing. All of life's problems are now washed away. Devotion and passion will always be present, and the desire to do what Jesus says will just come naturally. However, Peter's life counters those assumptions. When we look at Peter's life, we see a rocky up and down relationship with Jesus.

It was one of devotion, but it was also filled with doubt and denial.
There were times of passion, as well as times of plight.

Peter walked closely with the Lord, but he was often trying to make things happen on his own. When I look at a relationship like his, I see one like mine, and I believe I also see one like yours. This is why I have written this book. I want to look at things that are often overlooked. I want to reclaim the reality in relationships beyond feelings.

*Expectations are everything.*

I pray this book provides proper expectations that flourish your relationship with Jesus today, tomorrow, and for forever.

# [CHAPTER ONE]
## I Feel the Exact Same Way

*"I feel the exact same way."*

I will never forget sitting at Potbelly's on February 6, 2006 in Normal, Illinois, telling Jamie (my wife today) that I was interested in her and wanted to pursue her. I was so scared. I had absolutely no idea how she would respond. Would she feel the same way?

I remember sitting on my bed the night before, rehearsing how I was going to tell her that I wanted to take her on a date. I went through so many phrases and tried to pick the one that was the least dorky:

> *I like you.* (Sounds like we're in kindergarten.)
> *You're a lot of fun.* (Sounds even more like kindergarten.)
> *I'm attracted to you.* (Creepy if she didn't find me attractive, too.)
> *I had a dream that we were married.* (True, but definitely creepy!)

I even practiced different responses I would give to her possible responses! My default line if she said she had no interest in me was the infamous *Dumb and Dumber* line: "So you're saying there's still a chance!" Needless to say, I was a hopeless romantic and was praying she felt the same way about me that I felt about her.

Thankfully, she did. I told Jamie of my feelings for her, and her response was so simple, but so exciting:

*"I feel the exact same way."*

Immediately, I think I heard angels singing. Butterflies in my stomach began fluttering. Warm fuzzies, tingles, and goose bumps emerged. Surges of emotions burst forth like never before, and I was on cloud nine.

From that point forward, I was lovesick over Jamie. I always wanted to be with her, and tried my hardest to make every moment memorable. I sent meaningless texts to her when we were away from each other, and frequently canceled all other plans just to spend time with her.

I was crazy about her.

What else would you expect?

Have you ever fallen head over heels for someone?

Can you remember how it felt when you discovered he or she felt the exact same way you did?

**How do you think Jesus feels when you tell him that you feel the exact same way about him that he does about you?**

* * *

[ CHAPTER ONE // 15 ]

*Andrew, Simon Peter's brother, was one of the two who heard what John had said and who had followed Jesus. The first thing Andrew did was to find his brother Simon and tell him, "We have found the Messiah" (that is, the Christ). And he brought him to Jesus. Jesus looked at him and said, "You are Simon son of John. You will be called Cephas" (which, when translated, is Peter).*

*-John 1:40-42*

Everything suddenly shifted in Simon's life when his brother Andrew approached him and spoke these five simple words.

His life was forever changed.

Such a bold and provocative statement would have piqued any Jewish person's curiosity. For centuries, the Jewish people had longed for the coming of the Messiah. He was to be the anointed one that God promised to send to rescue them from their enemies, forgive them of their sins, and create for them a new beginning. Old Testament scriptures had been read in the synagogues filled of stories passed down through the generations about the coming Messiah.

He would come to make all things new.

We can just imagine the range of emotions that Simon must have felt when Andrew told him he had found the Messiah: his brother had essentially told him that he had found *the one*. These two words should quickly give us an idea of the emotions that went through Simon at that very moment.

*Have you ever thought that you may have found the one?*

*Were you not quickly filled with excitement and doubt?*

*Were you not filled with a surge of optimism and pessimism?*

*Was there not joy and fear welling up within you?*

[ 16 // THE DIP ]

Simon probably experienced the same type of mixed feelings leading him to investigate whether or not Jesus really was *the one*. So he went with Andrew to meet Jesus. While few specifics are given about their encounter, the main detail provided is significant. In his first meeting with Jesus, Simon was immediately given a new name.

*Why is this significant?*

In the Hebrew culture, a person's name was linked to their identity. A name was said to define who a person was.

For Simon, his name literally meant, "he has heard." Consider the appropriateness of this name. Simon had heard of the promised Messiah and longed for him to come just like the rest of the Jews. He had also now heard from his brother that they had found the Messiah. Simon had most definitely heard. However, Jesus immediately changed Simon's name to Cephas, which translated into English is the name Peter. This name means "rock."

In a matter of moments, the one who had heard was transformed into a potential rock of certainty.

Peter now began to believe he had found *the one* just like his brother.

After being renamed, Peter and a few others set out with Jesus for the next year or so on a preaching and healing tour throughout Israel. John 2:1-11 tells us their journey started at a wedding in the city of Cana where they watched Jesus turn water into wine.

They then made their way to Capernaum for a couple of days, and eventually went to Jerusalem for the Passover feast. Here, they watched Jesus make a whip of cords, overturn tables, and drive out money changers from the area of the Jewish temple set aside for the Gentiles to pray. All of this is recorded in John 2:12-25. These aggressive actions by Jesus likely brought to mind promises from Old Testament Scriptures like Psalm 69:9. This verse speaks of zeal for the house of God consuming the coming Messiah. After leaving Jerusalem, they headed back north through Samaria—an area most Jews stayed clear of because of a deep-seeded animosity between Jews and Samaritans. It could be compared to feuds between Israelis and Palestinians today. Nonetheless, Jesus not only traveled through the area, but he also stopped to speak to a Samaritan woman along the way telling her he was the promised Messiah. This absolutely startled those traveling with Jesus, including Peter.

Finally, they headed to back to the city of Cana. Upon arriving, Jesus healed the son of a Roman official. Both of these events are recorded in John 4.

Now, let's pause for a moment and put ourselves in the sandals of Peter throughout these remarkable experiences. If there had been any doubt in his mind when Andrew first approached him claiming he'd found the Messiah, it was now likely gone.

He had found the Messiah and was spending significant time with him.
He had witnessed the miracles with his own eyes.
He had walked from place to place with Jesus.
He had numerous conversations with him.

He had both heard and seen Jesus prove he was *the one*.
How incredible these moments had to have been for Peter!

Much like when we think we've found *the one* in dating, and feelings quickly spring up, the same was most likely true for Peter. He must have been on cloud nine. How many different times did he pinch himself along the way to see if he was dreaming? It probably felt so surreal.

Peter probably had a pounding heart, goose bumps, warm fuzzies, tingles, sweaty palms, and stuttering sentences at various times as he journeyed with Jesus. Peter was literally in close contact with *the one!*

Peter had just entered the honeymoon period of the relationship.

*The honeymoon period is the inaugural stage in a new relationship where feelings and infatuation take center stage; it's the dating-with-no-strings-attached point in the relationship.*

In the honeymoon period, everything is fresh and exhilarating! There's so much to be learned and discovered.

Optimism is prevalent and every moment is filled with potential.

We feel like we're on the top of a mountain as aspirations fill our hearts and dreams of grandeur dominate our thoughts.

Nothing seems impossible.

We feel like we can do anything because we've found *the one*.

Additionally, we find ourselves telling everyone we know about our new relationship. We're constantly belting out what's bursting from within us. And if people we tell don't agree with our new relationship, who cares?

No one can tell us any differently.

We're convinced that the feelings and the relationship will last forever.

In the honeymoon period, the level of commitment in the relationship is completely based on the intensity of the feelings.

If feelings are strong, the commitment is strong.
If feelings are weak, the commitment is weak.

The reality of what it takes to make a long-term committed relationship last is rarely considered.

The diagram on the next page graphs the honeymoon period as a steep incline with feelings as the foundation of that incline:

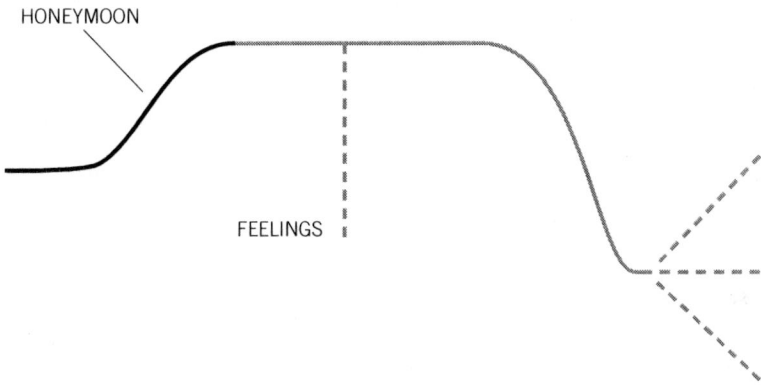

Feelings are the common and natural catalyst for initial commitment to a relationship. It is virtually impossible to steer clear of feelings as we attempt to make rational decisions. Emotions are always connected to initial commitment in some form or another.

For Peter, as well as for most people who find Jesus to be *the one*, feelings are certainly involved in the initial commitment. This is because the feelings within you come from God. He purposefully crafted us in such a way that feelings would be ignited when we experience Him and others. Part of being made in the image of God includes experiencing a range of feelings. One of the ways this is shown is in the life of Jesus. Feelings of the Son of God range from joy, to sadness, to celebration.

*And why wouldn't feelings be prominent when someone first accepts Christ?*

*How could an emotional response not have been prevalent in Peter's decision to follow Jesus?*

His life had just been completely changed. He had just been renamed. He was a brand new person.

The same is true for those today that give their lives to Jesus. The apostle Paul tells us in 2 Corinthians 5:17 that if anyone is in Christ, the old has gone, the new has come! We've been fully forgiven of all of our sins.

*How could we not be ecstatic, joyous, and a bit overwhelmed by such an amazing, life-changing, forever-altering promise?*

*How is it even possible that someone could be emotionally detached from such an incredible event?*

An emotional response is healthy because it allows us to exclaim and display what's going on inside of us. We can't keep it to ourselves. As C.S. Lewis says, "Joy is incomplete unless it's fully expressed."

I'll never forget the range of emotions I felt when I first met Jesus and committed my life to him. I had recently been arrested for drinking and driving, and a friend of mine invited me to come to his church. Little did I know at the time that this simple invitation would literally change my life now and forever. Being recently imprisoned and ashamed of my actions, I was much like the Jewish people that awaited a Messiah. I longed for someone to free me, forgive me, and give me a new future.

As music began playing at the church service, I was immediately overcome with emotion. The lyrics of the songs pierced my heart as they promised a way for new life through Jesus. I found myself in tears and not exactly knowing why. I was never a big crier, but I just couldn't hold them back.

After the music, the pastor got up to speak. I was blown away by what he said because I was convinced he must have spied on me throughout the week, for what he spoke about directly correlated to my life. I got tingles up the back of my neck because he was so dead-on. They finished with some more songs, but I couldn't sing.

I just sat in silence, completely overwhelmed with the message that God wanted a relationship with me.

It seemed surreal.

I continued going to church week after week, and each time I would experience the same feelings. I invited others to come with me, because I couldn't keep what I was feeling inside of me. No one could tell me any differently. The feelings had convinced me that God was real and in pursuit of me. I loved feeling the presence and closeness of God.

I couldn't get enough of the feelings.

Therefore, I decided to enter into a personal relationship with Jesus on March 7, 1999. Upon meeting Jesus, I was given a new identity just like Peter. I was no longer a sinner but a saint. The old had gone, and the new had come. I was a new creation in Christ. The honeymoon period was in full swing as I was blown away by the goodness and closeness of Christ.

I was infatuated with God and believed it would last forever.

This is the same phenomenon that takes place in the hearts of many new believers. They go to a worship service, summer camp, mission trip, concert, etc., and get so overwhelmed with emotions that they make a decision to follow God. In those moments, they are dead set on surrendering everything to Jesus. They enter into the honeymoon period believing the sensations will last forever.

For Peter and the gang, they believed they had found *the one* in a spiritual sense. It started with a simple invitation to come and see the alleged Messiah. There was little risk involved, but the potential payoff was incredible. For if Jesus really was the promised Messiah, everything was about to change!

Emotions flooded his heart and motivated him to commit to following Jesus throughout Israel with others who also were in the honeymoon period.

However, they didn't realize that when they got home, things would begin to change...

# [ CHAPTER TWO ]
## *So What Exactly Are We?*

*"So what exactly are we?"*

After going on a few dates with Jamie and having a great time, this was the question she asked. And when she did, I knew what it meant:

It was time for the DTR.
It was time to Define The Relationship!

For the past few weeks we had been cruising along in the relationship. We were having a blast, but there weren't really any strings attached yet, so to speak. Our time together had been very casual, fun, and exciting. We loved each other's company. Each night as I went to bed, I couldn't wait for whatever the next day had in store for the two of us.

Feelings were flowing, but commitment had yet to be verbalized.

It was assumed from the amount of time we had been spending with each other, but it had yet to be declared that we were "officially dating." In asking the question, Jamie wanted to know if we were or were not an item; she was essentially asking me if I was going to be exclusively committed to her.

The interesting thing about the DTR is that things will never be the same after you have it. In my mind, there are really only two options coming out of the DTR—make it official and commit, or end it.

The reason there are only two options is because feelings are transitioning into a need for exclusivity with the person who is initiating the DTR. He or she wants to know that the relationship is more than just "good times" at his or her expense.

They need to know that you desire to be in a committed relationship.

Thus, if you tell them you do want to be "official," you can move forward. However, if you're not ready to make it "official," it is directly interpreted as a rejection. And once that sentiment seeps into his or her mind, good luck trying to explain how that's not the case!

Thankfully, I was fully ready to have the DTR with Jamie and tell her that I would have it no other way but for us to be together. (In fact, our DTR went over so well, I asked her to marry me within two months!)

**What happens when Jesus is the one initiating the DTR with you?**

\* \* \*

> *As Jesus was walking beside the Sea of Galilee, he saw two brothers, Simon called Peter and his brother Andrew. They were casting a net into the lake, for they were fishermen. "Come, follow me," Jesus said, "and I will make you fishers of men." At once they left their nets and followed him. Going on from there, he saw two other brothers, James son of Zebedee and his brother John. They were in a boat with their father Zebedee, preparing their nets. Jesus called them, and immediately they left the boat and their father and followed him.*
>
> *- Matthew 4:18-22*

As highlighted in the previous chapter, Peter met Jesus and had a life-altering encounter with him. From that point on, Peter and the others traveled with Jesus for a little over a year throughout Israel. The experience had to have been breathtaking.

Not only did he witness miraculous feats firsthand, he also had the privilege of walking with the Son of God in close proximity. I would love to be able to listen in on the conversations they had as they walked from place to place.

I wonder about the questions Peter asked.

I wonder if Peter had that nervous, giddy feeling inside him every time Jesus addressed him personally.

I wonder if there were times when he felt he said something dumb, and then worried if Jesus would reconsider inviting him to travel with them.

I wonder if Peter always wanted to put his best foot forward because he feared Jesus would change his mind.

After the road trip ended, the Bible tells us that Jesus settled in Capernaum for a while. It is there we're told that Peter, his brother Andrew, and the sons of thunder (James and John) are fishing when Jesus comes calling. In Matthew 4:19, Jesus walks straight up to them on the shores of the Sea of Galilee and says, *"Come, follow me, and I will make you fishers of men."*

I'm not sure if or how this story was told to you as you were growing up, but this is how I was told the event went down: Jesus walked by the sea, called Peter and the gang, and they followed him because they recognized something special about Jesus. It was presented as if this were the first-ever encounter that Peter had with Jesus. Maybe Jesus was glowing or exuding an attractive odor or something, and that's why they were so in awe that they dropped their nets immediately and followed Jesus.

But this isn't the first time Jesus and Peter have met. It's actually far from the first time. They've known each other for a year now. A relationship has already been established, and both sides have already made investments into each other. Jesus has already changed his name from Simon to Peter.

Thus, when Jesus comes calling, he's initiating the DTR. Hanging out and spending significant time together for the past year has been nice, but now it's time to make it official—time to commit on the next level.

Jesus is essentially asking, *"So what exactly are we?"*

Peter makes the relationship official by dropping his nets and following Jesus. But once a DTR happens and we fully commit to the relationship, things have the potential to change greatly. The carefree, no strings attached spirit of the relationship is now met with expectations and some boundaries.

In most cases, if the DTR yields a defined relationship, there's another surge of emotion. Feelings intensify yet again because of the excitement that comes with being "official." However, over the course of time after the DTR, that intensity begins to simmer down.

And it's here that Peter has entered the plateau period of the relationship.

*The plateau period is the point when emotions that initially sprung from the newness of a relationship slowly become less intense.* It's the point in the relationship when you begin asking all sorts of questions.

*Why don't I feel the same way anymore?*

*Why don't I feel as close to God as I did a few months ago?*

*Was what I originally felt not legitimate?*

The plateau period is the point when feelings become less prominent and the reality of the commitment sets in. In the honeymoon phase, the reality of the commitment wasn't truly considered because things were primarily based upon feelings and experiences. However, in the plateau period, reality joins with emotions, and we may begin to consider what we've gotten ourselves into regarding this relationship.

Questions emerge.

The opinions of others that never mattered start to.

Practical concerns arise.

Sacrifice is no longer a foreign term, because now that the relationship is official, you must give up certain things to make the relationship work. All in all, there's simply a higher level of commitment than there was in the honeymoon stage.

This causes us to press in and consider if the relationship is worth it.

The plateau period is a vital stage in every relationship, but many don't know what to do when they enter into it, because love is generally equated with feelings alone.

However, love is so much more than just feelings.

The diagram on the next page graphs the plateau period as a straight line with feelings as a part of the foundation, but now with commitment coming into the picture, too.

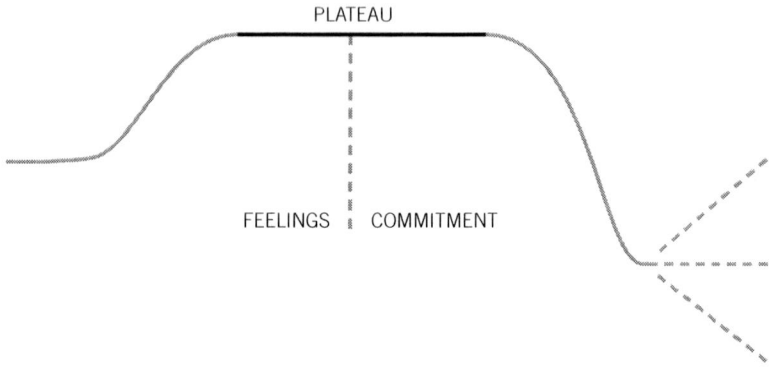

Upon marrying my wife, my feelings continued to surge, but as time passed, there were days that my feelings just weren't as intense as they were when I asked her to be my bride. Now, if I had gone into marriage without realistic expectations that this was completely normal, I would have been extremely worried. I would have figured that since there wasn't a yearning to make every moment memorable that something was wrong.

However, this is just the way of marriage, and any relationship for that matter. Sometimes there are huge goose bumps and swarming butterflies, but there are also times when goose bumps aren't so bumpy and the butterflies seem to have gone into their winter cocoons.

This may sound sad if you've never been in a long-term relationship or marriage, but for those that are married, you know what I'm saying is true. My wife would say the exact same thing. We have an absolutely remarkable marriage, and make no mistake about it—I'm crazy in love with her. But there are times when we're on the tops of mountains, and there are times when we're just married. Both are ok because every relationship comes to a point when feelings have to take a back seat to commitment. It doesn't mean feelings are abandoned altogether, but there is a realization that commitment and sacrifice are the real determiners of true love.

The same dynamics that characterize my relationship with my wife also take place in a relationship with Jesus. Initially, there's the onslaught of emotion described in the previous chapter, but as the relationship progresses, those emotions sometimes surface, but at other times lie dormant.

Worship services are still impactful, but we may no longer find ourselves with tears streaming down our faces.

Sermons may still resonate, but not as if they were given to the pastor from God because they parallel every aspect of our lives.

Lies can fill our minds because we're not used to worshiping God without an overwhelming feeling of ecstasy. We may find ourselves assuming that God is no longer close, that we must have sinned too much. Or maybe you did something to offend God, causing him to back away rather than draw near.

But nothing could be further from the truth.

God is still active in our lives and just as near to us now as he was when we first gave our lives to him; the difference is that the feelings have started to fade, and commitment must now kick in. If we have unrealistic expectations that there must be an emotional rush to know that God is with us, then now is the time to realize that this is simply unrealistic. Similar to how there are days when we're just married, sometimes there are days that we're just being faithful to God even though we don't feel him.

It's the nature of relationship.

In fact, if we study Scripture closely, the longer people follow Christ, fewer miracles are prominent as faithfulness, sacrifice, and commitment come to the forefront. Take a quick survey of the book of Acts and you'll see that miracles, signs, and wonders are emphasized in the lives of apostles the first sixteen chapters, but then a transition takes place.

The remaining twelve chapters focus less on the miraculous and more on the apostles living out their faith in Jesus. Simply, the relationship matures from relying on God because of what God does, to living for God because of who God is.

This is the same as our significant others wanting to know we love them for who they are, not just what they do. The same is true for God. God wants us to love him because he has the power to change lives and perform miracles, but he also wants us to love him simply because he's God.

In the life of Peter, while the plateau stage isn't directly referred to, it can be inferred. Upon Jesus' call to drop their nets and follow, Peter and the other three disciples commit to Jesus. From that moment on, they travel with Jesus throughout the Galilee area witnessing his reputation grow more and more as the crowds grow larger and larger. They also began facing opposition from the religious leaders of the day. These leaders didn't take a liking to Jesus as the crowds did, probably due to the fact that Jesus continually exposed them for what they were—hypocrites.

Peter and the others traveling with Jesus also saw him perform more and more miracles from healing all types of diseases, to driving demons out of people, to even silencing a mighty thunderstorm. As with the previous tour, this had to have been an incredible experience for his disciples.

However, the question I can't help asking is whether or not witnessing the healings and other miracles Jesus performed were as spectacular the second, third, fourth, and fifth times around?

I imagine each time Peter witnessed a miraculous healing it was truly astounding, but with each successive miracle, I wonder if it became more and more of the same.

It became the norm.
 …familiar.
 …routine.

I wonder this because I believe this happens often in our lives. New eventually becomes old, and old eventually becomes boring.

As Peter continued traveling with Jesus, I am sure that he absolutely loved it, but also that he likely began wondering when Jesus would do the things God promised: rescue the Jews from their enemies, forgive them of their sins, and create a whole new future for them. Jesus was performing miracles but what about salvation? Remember, expectations are everything and when expectations are not met, disappointment and frustration leave us questioning what we thought we knew.

For Peter, the more time he spent with Jesus, the more he likely became confused because his initial expectations were not being met.

Plus, Peter was a Jewish boy. He would have grown up under the teachings of the religious leaders that Jesus was now calling into question. This had to have caused some doubts in Peter's mind as to whether or not this relationship was worth the cost. While it still felt good most of the time, there were probably more moments of negativity. At times, it was actually becoming more difficult.

This was much different than the way things started for Peter and Jesus.

How would Peter handle the difficulty, transition, and opposition?

Would Peter stick to his commitment made with the DTR, or would he succumb to the Dip?

## [ CHAPTER THREE ]
### *You've Changed*

*"You've changed."*

While these two words can sometimes be spoken as encouragement, that wasn't Jamie's purpose when she said them to me a few years into our marriage. She was referring to the fact that early on in our marriage, I was quick to offer her affection. Specifically, I never complained about massaging her back and shoulders, running my fingers through her hair, and gently tickling her forearms.

In the beginning...I did them without her asking.

Now...Jamie had to ask for me to do them.

And when she asked, I generally complained before complying.
This is what brought about her startling statement:

*"You've changed."*

These two words implied so much when she said them to me. They implied that I no longer cared as much about her, and that she didn't like the

Brandon that was sitting in front of her. Rather, she desired the Brandon that would offer her affection without her having to ask for it. The problem was that since I didn't desire this kind of affection or feel that I needed it, I assumed Jamie didn't need it any longer either. Wrong! Jamie still wanted as much affection as she did when we first got married.

Initially, when Jamie spoke these words to me, I lashed back defensively. I insisted I never lavished her with affection early on in our relationship, but she knew better—and I knew better, too! The moment that defensiveness came out as my initial response, I knew she was right.

The best way to know if someone else is right is when he or she strikes a nerve within you that elicits defensiveness.

The truth can hurt.

After I finally acknowledged that she was right, I asked for forgiveness and did my best to improve my affection output, and continue to do so today.

The point is that I hated that I had changed for the worse, not for the better. I made a promise to Jamie the day we got married that I would always cherish and serve her, no matter what.

I promised I would sacrifice my needs to meet her needs.
She promised me likewise.

Yet here was an example of me not living out my promise.

In that moment, Jamie brought me back to my original calling.

**What happens when Jesus is the one reminding us to live the way we promised?**

* * *

[ CHAPTER THREE // 35 ]

> *One day as Jesus was standing by the Lake of Gennesaret, with the people crowding around him and listening to the word of God, he saw at the water's edge two boats, left there by fishermen, who were washing their nets. He got into one of the boats, the one belonging to Simon, and asked him to put out a little from shore. Then he sat down and taught the people from the boat. When he had finished speaking, he said to Simon, "Put out into deep water, and let down the nets for a catch."*
>
> *- Luke 5:1-4*

At the end of Luke 4, we are told that after the healing of Peter's mother-in-law, crowds began to bombard Jesus to the point that he had to find a solitary place. And even there, the crowds pursued him. Thus, Jesus says in verse 43, *"I must preach the good news of the kingdom of God to the other towns also, because this is why I was sent."* He then continued preaching in the synagogues of Judea. Finally, Jesus left the city of Capernaum and went to other cities.

But the big question that must be answered is this: *Where is Peter?*

It appears that Jesus goes to these places and Peter does not join him.

How is this possible?

The last time we saw Peter, he had dropped his nets to follow Jesus and fish for men. I thought he had responded affirmatively to the DTR and made it official with Jesus.

If so, why isn't Peter with Jesus?

In Luke 5, we have a fascinating account of Jesus coming once again to the Sea of Galilee and calling the first disciples. For centuries, debate has centered on whether or not this passage is the same account of Jesus calling Peter and the three others in Matthew 4:18-22 and Mark 1:14-20. I am convinced this is a completely different account because the details are too different.

In Matthew and Mark's accounts, Jesus walks down the shore of Galilee and sees Peter and Andrew casting their nets into the lake, while Luke's episode has the two washing their nets. Additionally, Luke's gospel goes into great detail about a huge catch of fish that we'll explore later in this chapter. Matthew and Mark fail to even mention this miraculous catch.

What we see in Matthew 4 and Mark 1 is Jesus calling Peter to follow.

What we see in Luke 5 is Jesus *re*-calling Peter to follow because Peter has hit the Dip.

The incident began with Jesus standing by the Lake of Gennesaret, another name for the Sea of Galilee, presumably having recently returned from his trip to several cities throughout Judea. There were people gathered around Jesus listening to him as he taught the Word of God. Evidently, the people were not respectful of personal space, because Jesus found a couple of boats on the water's edge and got into one of them.

The boat Jesus chose belonged to Peter.

Jesus proceeds to ask Peter to move the boat from the shore into the water so he can teach the people without being crowded.

While the text does not directly tell us this, we know the time of day is the early morning because Peter and others are washing their nets, revealing that they've just gotten back from an all-nighter of fishing.

Because of this, Peter is exhausted.

But more than that—he's busted!

You see, it's very easy at this point to continue reading about what happens next, but we shouldn't just gloss over the fact that Peter is fishing.

Wasn't he supposed to be following Jesus?

Hadn't Jesus called him away from fishing for fish so that he could fish for men?

This had to have been such an awkward moment for Peter: he's gone back to fishing rather than following, and the very next morning, Jesus shows up on the shoreline wanting to use his boat.

Is this not the story of so many of our spiritual lives?

The same question asked of Peter should be asked of us, too.

We all too often go back to fishing in our everyday lives.

We say yes to Jesus and begin the journey, but somewhere along the way, we find ourselves gravitating back to the life we allegedly left behind.

Why are we a people that so often choose *fishing* instead of *following?*

I believe the answer is because we're naïve when it comes to understanding the Dip—the point in every relationship when feelings fade as the core foundational piece of commitment takes its rightful place.

The Dip is that point when it becomes more about the other person than it does you.

It's when the reality sets in of what it's actually going to take for the relationship to work—selflessness and sacrifice.

When the Dip hits, the question we find ourselves asking over and over again is whether or not the relationship is worth staying in. In a culture that paints the picture of commitment defined by sticking around the morning after, the idea of actually staying in a relationship for the long haul is becoming an increasingly foreign concept.

It's just easier to start all over, as opposed to working through things.

Additionally, we live in a time of awareness and options. Like no other period in human history, we're constantly exposed to various ideas and opportunities that we can easily adopt if we want to. This ranges from relationships, to occupations, to possessions, to religious faiths, to ice cream flavors.

In churches, this ranges from musical worship styles, to preaching preferences, to kids ministry, to small groups, to stances on divorce and homosexuality. You name it, there's an opinion and an option, making it even more difficult to consider choosing just one.

Awareness always births discontentment.

Therefore, we find ourselves constantly discontented with what we have, who we're with, and what we're doing, because we see the plethora of options right in front of us, or with the click of a mouse.

The diagram below graphs the Dip as a steep decline because feelings are not the driving force, but rather the reality of commitment has come to the forefront.

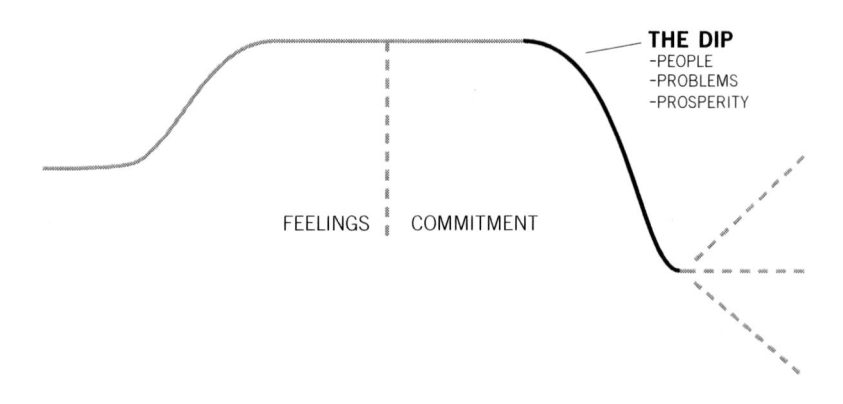

**THE DIP**
-PEOPLE
-PROBLEMS
-PROSPERITY

FEELINGS | COMMITMENT

While there are a variety of things that can cause the Dip to hit in our lives, there are three primary areas that bring about the Dip:

People…Problems…Prosperity

These three areas can be seen in Peter's Dip and give us an indication of why he (and often we) choose to go back to fishing rather than following.

\* \* \*

### THE PEOPLE DIP

Fishing was Peter's livelihood. It was how he made money and put food on the table. This is extremely important to note, considering Peter was married. When Peter chose to drop his nets and follow, he was essentially walking away from his ability to make money.

If you're married, you know right away how well it would go over with your spouse if you came home and told her you were leaving your job so you could follow a guy around claiming he was the Son of God.

We can't know for sure, but I'm willing to bet there may have been some strife at home when Peter shared this news with his wife. You've got to think that at some point a conversation took place about how they were going to make ends meet if he was quitting his job.

And if the conversation wasn't between Peter and his wife, I would bet my life it took place at some point between Peter and his in-laws. I can just hear the questions aimed at Peter about how he expected to provide for their daughter by following an alleged Messiah around, rather than fishing.

Perhaps this is why Jesus chose to heal Peter's mother-in-law during the second preaching and healing tour.

Perhaps Jesus healed Peter's mother-in-law to affirm to her that he would take care of everything, and she need not worry.

Along with the pressure Peter was likely getting from his wife and in-laws, others would have been giving him grief over his decision to follow Jesus, too. Remember that while Jesus was gaining momentum, as seen in the crowds of people coming to hear him teach and be healed, there were also many skeptics. Jesus was not the first to come during that time claiming he was the Messiah. There were others who made the same bold proclamation.

Additionally, the prominent religious leaders of the day were not fans of Jesus. They opposed his teachings and told others that he was not to be followed. Growing up in the Jewish way of life, Peter would have been brought up to respect the Torah, as well as the Tradition of the Elders. The Torah is the first five books of the Old Testament—Genesis, Exodus, Leviticus, Numbers, and Deuteronomy. The Tradition of the Elders was a compilation of interpretations of the Torah by rabbis throughout the centuries. These interpretations were later made into the Mishnah.

Therefore, it's fair to assume a battle took place both internally and externally about whether or not Jesus was a legitimate candidate to be the long awaited Messiah.

Should Peter follow the instruction of religious leaders he grew up listening to, or should he put his full trust in the words of Jesus, who often spoke counter to the religious leaders?

If you've ever been in a relationship, you know exactly what outside pressure can do to your relationship. If someone is constantly pessimistic about your relationship, eventually you may question your commitment.

In the honeymoon stage, the opinions of other people don't matter much because your feelings overcome criticism or questioning. However, once you reach the plateau period, your ears suddenly open up to the voices of others. What they say suddenly matters and can quickly cause you to plummet into the Dip.

I know so many people that have given their lives to following Jesus who initially didn't care what others had to say. But after some time had passed, the questions, criticisms, and doubts of family and friends started to become their own questions, criticisms, and doubts. The rejection they received from others started to cause them to reject Jesus. It would just be easier not to follow Him and appease the voices in the crowd.

Perhaps this is why Peter has returned to fishing.

In Matthew 13:1-23, Mark 4:1-20, and Luke 8:1-15, Jesus gives a famous parable that alludes to the three causes for the Dip. Peter would have been very familiar with this parable because theologians believe Jesus taught it frequently as he traveled to different places preaching and teaching.

The parable tells of a farmer who went out to sow his seed. As he scattered the seed, some fell on the path, some on the rock, some on thorns, and some fell on good soil. Jesus then shared what happened to the seed as it fell on the different surfaces. The first of those surfaces that the seed fell upon was the path. The parable says the seed that fell upon the path never made it because it was trampled upon, and the birds of the air ate it up.

Later when the disciples ask Jesus the meaning of the parable, he explains that the seed falling upon the path is representative of those who hear, but from whom the devil takes the word, so they will not believe and be saved.

One way the devil so often comes and snatches up the Word of God from our lives is through the voices of others. This is what causes the people Dip. Whether they are skeptical, sarcastic, pessimistic, or cynical, such voices cause commitment to be questioned.

We're a people who care deeply about what others think, so when others question us, it's easier to conform rather than press on.

The chirping of hungry birds gets the best of us. We allow them to come and eat up the seed of faith and commitment we originally subscribed to when we said yes to following Jesus.

There are so many people out there who walk away from relationships (both with people and with Christ) because we listen to the wrong voices:

> the voices of jealous friends who want more of our time that's now devoted to church-related activities and Christian friends…

> the voices of protective family members who don't understand why we choose to spend so much time reading our Bibles or worrying about others rather than looking out for ourselves…

> the voices of condescending professors who insist that the idea of God is foolish and a huge waste of time, because science and technology have proven God doesn't exist and isn't needed…

> the voices of greedy bosses who demand more work, forcing you to be away from your family, and miss going to church…

> the voices of charming men and seductive women who promise us that the way they make us feel will actually last…

> the voices of disgruntled former churchgoers that bash the church because it's full of hypocrites showing that God can't change lives…

> the voices of social media, movies, and music that generally only tell us half-truths, making destructive promises disguised by incredible editing…

*Whose voice is easiest for you to listen to?*

All of these voices and many, many more have the potential to bring about the people Dip. They strike a chord with our soul's deep desire for acceptance, so we do whatever we can to fit in and be accepted.

Sadly, the voice that matters most, the one who accepts us no matter what, is the voice we choose to drown out.

**Can you resonate with the people Dip?**

## THE PROBLEM DIP

The problem Dip is likely another reason that Peter went back to fishing instead of following. We're told in Luke 5:4 that Jesus asked Peter to take the boat out a ways from shore and cast the nets into deep water to catch some fish. Such a request would have tested every bit of patience Peter possessed, considering he and the others had been out all night and were unsuccessful.

Peter tells Jesus in verse 5:5,
 *"Master, we've worked hard all night and haven't caught anything."*

Put yourself in this moment for just a second. Peter is an accomplished fisherman. He has his own fishing business with his brother Andrew, and possibly James and John, too. Fishing is what he knows. It's what he's good at. It comes effortlessly to him.

At this point, Peter's just spent an entire night fishing and has caught nothing. He's ready to call it a day, go home, and get some sleep. But Jesus has other plans. Jesus, a carpenter by trade, comes on the scene and tells Peter to get the boat back out on the water and try again.

What might go through your mind if you were Peter in this moment?

My thoughts might have gone a little something like this:

> *Alright Jesus, here's the deal—my guys and I are professionals. We know what we're doing. The best time to fish is at night, not in the morning. We just got back from a long night with nothing to show for it, so let's not waste our time going back out. Take my word on this one Jesus—it's not worth heading back out there. You stick to carpentry, preaching, teaching, and healing, but leave the fishing to me.*

Ultimately, Peter's problem is more than just exhaustion. His primary problem is that he hasn't caught any fish. The ramification of this would be another day's wages lost. He's already taken a pay cut following Jesus around, and now that he's returned to make some money, he isn't successful.

This causes Peter to experience a problem Dip. He's left wondering if God is truly a provider who is able to get him through this dilemma.

An image that comes to mind is a scene from the movie *The Pursuit of Happyness,* when Will Smith's character continues returning home with the bone graph scanner machines that he is trying to sell. His wife is furious because each unsuccessful sale means more stress for their family.

Problems frequently cause a Dip in our commitment to Christ. Problems can range from the loss of a job, leading to a struggle to make ends meet; to simply reading the frequent headlines highlighting the latest tragedy, murder, earthquake, tornado, volcanic eruption, genocide, scandal, rape, affair, divorce, you name it.

Such problems cause us to question the presence, provision, and ultimately, the goodness of God.

When problems come our way, they can be an automatic excuse to walk away from Jesus and go back to leading our own life rather than trusting God.

Problems rock us so much because they don't feel good.
Shocking, but true.

> We don't know how to deal with negative feelings because we're positive emotion addicts, evidenced by the honeymoon stage.
>
> We don't know how to deal with the feelings that come when we hear the news of a loved one getting cancer.
>
> We don't know how to deal with the negative feelings that come when we've been betrayed, backstabbed, or cheated on.

We don't know how to deal with the shocking images of poverty, despair, and death that come when natural disasters wreak havoc on a particular area.

So when problems crash down and negative emotions flood in, the Dip hits hard.

In Jesus' parable, the second type of surface the seed fell upon was rock. The seed grew into plant life, but it withered when it came up because it had no moisture. Jesus later explains to his disciples that this represents those who receive the word with joy when they hear it, but it is without root.

Therefore, they believe for awhile, but in the time of testing, they fall away.

The testing is what births the problem Dip; there's an initial reception to the word of God, with a surge of joy and strong emotion. Big promises are made, but over the course of time, joy diminishes and the word goes by the wayside. Much like what was mentioned in the introduction, the joy often gets stripped away because of unrealistic expectations we have when we enter into a relationship with Jesus.

Sadly, today there are so many distorted theologies being promoted that tell us that a relationship with Christ equals the absence of problems. Since Jesus makes all things new, this must include the problems we deal with day to day. So when problems continue to come our way, we don't know how to deal with them. We assume that either our decision was not legitimate, or that the God we put our faith in is no longer worth it if he's not able to rid us of our problems.

The problem Dip can so easily get the best of us.

Those who ascribe to this type of theology need only hear the words of Jesus in John 16:33,

*"I have told you these things, so that in me you may have peace. In this world you will have trouble. But take heart! I have overcome the world."*

The promise of this verse is the presence of peace, not the absence of problems. Jesus brings peace that endures through our problems. However, the beautiful and ultimate hope of Christ is found in the last words of that same verse as he promises that a day is coming when he will overcome the world.

The destructive warpath of sin will come to an end.

Jesus will overcome.

Those who have placed their faith in him will be victorious with him.

Take heart!

In our marriage, Jamie and I have had our fair share of issues, from petty to pressing. On the petty side of things, we've argued over how towels should be folded to how the house should be cleaned. On the pressing side, we've wrestled through the deaths of loved ones, as well as friends walking away from Christ.

With all of these problems, we could just throw in the towel, but we hold to Jesus' promise that in this life there will be trouble. We also seek the peace Jesus promises and cling to the truth that he will overcome!

**Can you resonate with the problem Dip?**

* * *

### *THE PROSPERITY DIP*

The last Dip Peter experiences in Luke 5 is the prosperity Dip—the subtlest and most seductive of the three. Jesus, the Son of God, called Peter to follow him and become a fisher of men. This is essentially a call to use his gifts not only for his sake, but also for the sake of the kingdom of God.

This is why God gives us gifts—to provide for our needs, but also to use those gifts to provide for the needs of others, so that they might see the goodness and provision of God.

But here we have Peter again fishing for fish instead of men, as Jesus had called him to do. Why is this? Why wouldn't Peter do what Jesus asked? Why wouldn't he trust Jesus to provide for him, considering Jesus was the maker of heaven and earth? That alone should give Peter reason enough to trust in Jesus' ability to provide.

But what if Peter's return to fishing isn't so much about needing provision as it is about wanting *more* provision?

What if Peter is already fully provided for, yet he just wants more?

He wants more fish because this would mean more money.
More money would bring greater potential to buy more things.
More things would be seen as more security and possible notoriety.

Perhaps Peter's return to fishing was driven not as much by doubt as it was by greed.

*More.*

This is the word that drives so many of our lives. We always want *more*. We're never satisfied with what we have. We may be satisfied for a few moments, days, or weeks, but eventually our appetites for more drive us to consume. In our culture, people are constantly in a state of want, but often blinded to the reality that we already have everything we need.

We have a desire to acquire and this appetite is heightened by what we see all around us. People are always consuming—food, clothes, sex, entertainment, relationships, property, cell phones, success, money, fame, etc. We are so hungry for more, but we really don't know what exactly it is we're hungry for. So we just consume anything and everything we possibly can.

When Jesus called Peter to follow him, he was inviting him into the fulfillment of the craving for more. The same is true for us.

Jesus invites us to be satisfied fully in him.

Many of us understand that initially when we accept Christ. We find ourselves amazed with the grace and peace that fills our hearts, and for a time, the drive for more subsides. Over time though, rather than craving more grace and peace from Jesus, we again crave temporal things that can't satisfy.

Living in America, the wealthiest nation in the world, fans the flame of greed more than any other place on the planet ever could. We have everything we could possibly ever need, yet amazingly, advertisements and media continually convince us that we still need more. Thus, we find ourselves pulling up a seat around the table of consumption, joining the rest of the country in the lie of consumerism. And when we do, the grace and peace that entered our hearts when we first experienced Christ slowly fades away.

Or as Jesus said—it gets choked out.

The third kind of soil that Jesus references in his parable about a farmer scattering seed was the ground covered with thorns. The seed grew into a plant amongst the thorns, which eventually choked out the plant by soaking up all of its necessary moisture. Jesus says the thorns represent those who hear, but as they begin their spiritual journey are choked by life's worries, riches, and pleasures, and will not mature.

Choked…

Riches…

Pleasures…

These three words grab my attention because rarely do we associate riches and pleasures with choking. Generally, we associate them with satisfaction. However, this is the exact opposite of what Jesus teaches. Riches and pleasures put a stranglehold on us and cause us to lose perspective on what really matters.

While riches and pleasures are not evil in and of themselves, sin perverts them to the point that they choke out the word of God sown in our hearts. We must be aware of this and be on guard. In Luke 12:15 Jesus himself says in one of his teachings,

> *"Watch out! Be on your guard against all kinds of greed; a man's life does not consist in the abundance of his possessions."*

Jesus was fully aware of the sexiness of consumerism.

We must be, too.

The reason the prosperity Dip is so subtle is because it's a blind Dip. Wealth and possessions steal our hearts away from Jesus, and we often don't even realize it. We're sinking fast yet have no clue how far down we've sunk.

The most destructive part of the prosperity Dip is that money and possessions decrease our dependence on the Heavenly Father to provide. Since we now have the power to provide for ourselves, we look less to Jesus. Although God was the first giver of gifts, we hijack what he's given, and use them for our own gain rather than for the sake of his Kingdom. And before we know it, the prosperity Dip steals our souls, and we find ourselves fishing, and fishing, and fishing some more.

But in the end, we are left as Peter was when he told Jesus, "We've caught nothing."

This is what the prosperity Dip brings us—nothing.

Not more.

*Nothing.*

**Can you resonate with the prosperity Dip?**

\* \* \*

Jesus' parable concludes with a final possibility. The surface the seed that prospered fell upon was good soil. When the seed fell upon the good soil, plants came up that yielded a crop a hundred times more than what was sown. Jesus then explained that the good soil represents those who hear the word, retain it, and through perseverance, produce a bountiful crop.

The good soil is what Jesus was calling Peter to be.

The good soil is what Jesus is calling us to be.

However, what if the Dip has hardened our hearts, causing the word to be trampled upon, snatched away, or choked out, like it was with Peter?

Thus, the question you may be thinking is simply this:

*How do we get through the Dip?*

The answer to this question lies in a word mentioned in Jesus' explanation of the parable, and it's where we turn our attention as we see how the rest of the story plays out in Luke 5.

# [ CHAPTER FOUR ]
## We're Rich in Love

*"We're rich in love."*

During our first year of marriage, Jamie said this one day when we were surveying our completely bare living room. It was just a carpeted floor with windows and a fireplace. There were neither curtains to accent the windows or furniture to accent the room.

As we were laughing about how we had just hosted twenty college leaders from the ministry I pastor, and had to ask them to sit on the floor, telling them that our next investment would be furniture, Jamie looked at me and said, "We're rich in love."

Phrases like this are why I'm crazy about my wife.

We immediately coined the phrase and every time we would see something we wanted, but didn't need or couldn't afford, we'd look at each other and say, *"We're rich in love."*

The reason I love this phrase so much is because of what lies beneath it. Beneath the phrase are promises that I hold to dearly.

…the promise that I matter to my wife more than possessions.
…the promise that I alone am satisfying to her, no matter what.
…the promise that she'll stick with me through thick and thin.

And while it was just furniture and curtains we were referring to that day, the sentiment carries over into every area of our marriage. Because we're rich in love—true love—we're going to make it.

Jamie is not going to quit loving me because of other *people*.
Jamie is not going to quit loving me because we have *problems*.
Jamie is not going to quit loving me because of increasing *prosperity*.

We're in this thing to the end because we're rich in the greatest and deepest of ways—we're rich in love!

**Would you stick with Jesus if you could fully fathom that he is rich in love toward you, no matter what?**

\* \* \*

[ CHAPTER FOUR // 53 ]

*Simon answered, "Master, we've worked hard all night and haven't caught anything. But because you say so, I will let down the nets." When they had done so, they caught such a large number of fish that their nets began to break. So they signaled their partners in the other boat to come and help them, and they came and filled both boats so full that they began to sink.*

*When Simon Peter saw this, he fell at Jesus' knees and said, "Go away from me, Lord; I am a sinful man!" For he and all his companions were astonished at the catch of fish they had taken, and so were James and John, the sons of Zebedee, Simon's partners. Then Jesus said to Simon, "Don't be afraid; from now on you will fish for people."*

*So they pulled their boats up on shore, left everything and followed him.*
*- Luke 5:5-11*

If the last words of Peter had been a complaint when Jesus asked him to put his nets back out into the water after fishing all night and catching nothing, then he would never have seen what happened next. After expressing his frustration, Peter then proceeded to say in Luke 5:5,

*"But because you say so, I will let down my nets."*

I like to call this reluctant obedience. You can almost feel the emotion behind Peter's words here. It's like a child that's just been asked to do something he doesn't want to do, but complies only because it's his father asking him to do it.

Although Peter had hit the Dip, he still had trust and belief in the words of Jesus. His faith wasn't completely gone. This is often the exact same truth about many of us when we hit the Dip. Thankfully for Peter, he reluctantly obeyed Jesus' request, and this obedience seems to have pulled him through the Dip.

Upon lowering the nets, Peter is met with an astonishing, heart-realigning surprise. As opposed to catching nothing like the entire night before, the nets fill with fish to the breaking point! If Peter had been worried about providing for his family, that burden was gone. This huge catch would mean a huge payday for Peter!

Can you imagine the excitement, amazement, and humility that would flood your heart in this moment if you were Peter?

Much like how someone may commit to making a relationship official, only to back out a few weeks later because of fear and uncertainty, and then realize they've made a huge mistake backing out—Peter asks for forgiveness for not fulfilling his promise to follow Jesus. It was almost like Jesus knew what the reason was for Peter not following him: he knew Peter struggled with people, problems, and prosperity. This huge catch immediately provided for all of these needs in Peter.

Peter was so overwhelmed that he fell to his knees and immediately asked Jesus for forgiveness. *"Go away from me, Lord; I am a sinful man!"*

Now why would Peter make this statement knowing that Jesus hadn't said anything about his sin?

I believe it's because he understands himself enough to know that when Jesus offers him this lavish gift of undeserved grace, he can't help but acknowledge his own wickedness. His true motives for going back to fishing were exposed.

This is the way grace works.
It reveals our true self.

Peter is so ashamed that he asks Jesus to go away from him. This is such a tender, vulnerable, and beautiful moment. The next words that leave Jesus' mouth in response to Peter's confession are words that all of us who have Dipped must take to heart. Jesus had the right to say something like the following to Peter:

*You're absolutely right, Peter. You are a sinful man. You should be ashamed of yourself. What were you possibly thinking? Here's the fish you wanted so badly, but now I'm out of here. I'm going to invest my time in someone that will actually trust and appreciate me.*

But this is not even close to what Jesus says to Peter. Rather, Jesus simply looks upon the broken man and says, *"Don't be afraid; from now on you will catch men."* Talk about grace! I can't get enough of these words!

Jesus doesn't give up on Peter; he gives Peter a fresh start once again…

Peter, don't be afraid about providing for your family.
*I'll take care of it.*

Peter, don't be afraid of others and what they're saying about you.
*I love you.*

Peter, don't be afraid of not having enough.
*I am all you need.*

Peter, don't be afraid of tarnishing your reputation.
*You are mine.*

Peter, don't be afraid of walking away from what's comfortable.
*I'm with you.*

Peter, don't be afraid of all that you don't know.
*I'll lead you.*

Peter, don't be afraid of what you've done in the past.
*I've forgiven you.*

In an instant, Jesus reclaims Peter with the same call he had given him a few months previously.

Peter's Dip did not forfeit his calling.

This is pivotal because so many of us often believe our struggle through the Dip ultimately strips away any possibility of Jesus using us in the future. Nothing could be further from the truth, seen as Jesus *re*-calls Peter.

Jesus essentially comes to Peter and tells him that he's rich in love, a love that can endure through anything and everything—even the Dip.

The text goes on to tell us in verse 11 that Peter and the guys pulled their boats up to the shore, *left everything*, and followed Jesus. These two words are imperative because in their first encounter they dropped their nets and followed Jesus (Matthew 4:20).

This time they *left everything*.

It's almost like the author is ensuring that we realize that at first, Peter walked away from some things, but not everything. However, this time around, Peter didn't just drop his nets.

He *left everything* and followed.

In this moment, Peter pushed past his feelings to enter into a true, committed relationship with Jesus. True commitment is seen when we actually give our lives away to someone else because we trust them completely. This is what Peter does through his obedience, and it pulls him out of the Dip.

Such a decision shows he's trusting and depending on Christ, no matter what. In the parable that we looked at in the previous chapter, Jesus concluded by calling us to be the good soil upon which the Word of God can fall on, take root, and grow up to produce a crop a hundred times more than what is sown. But if we look at the parable closely, there's a word that's key and should shape all of our expectations when entering into any relationship—and especially a relationship with Jesus.

In order for the good soil to become a vast crop, we're told that perseverance is necessary (Luke 8:15). Perseverance is the key element of true love.

It's also the call Jesus has given each and every one of us who follow Him.

We are to persevere.

There are three options that can come from a Dip in our faith:
(1) To persevere, (2) to conform, or (3) to quit.

As I've already said, the Dip is an inevitable part of every relationship, because true commitment outlasts emotional highs. Since feelings fade and don't remain as intense as they initially were, perseverance is vitally important to adopt as a discipline when we enter into any relationship.

But before hammering home why perseverance is essential, let's first look at why quitting and conforming are other possibilities that come out of the Dip, but should be avoided at all costs.

* * *

## QUITTING

Quitting is self-explanatory.

As evidenced by the divorce rate, decreasing church attendance, and declining numbers of those that identify themselves as Christians in this country, quitting is something the Dip causes many people to do.

Instead of pushing through and trying to work things out, it's just easier to start all over.

Most that quit do so because they're looking for the honeymoon stage all over again, complete with warm fuzzies, tingles, and goose bumps. They yearn for the feeling of love and newness, so they make changes to re-enter the honeymoon stage.

This is why people have affairs, change jobs, switch majors, try new sports, and so on.

In the end, people that choose to quit do so because they've chosen feeling good over commitment. They then find themselves in a vicious, never-ending cycle of trying new things, yet never being satisfied, only to end up empty.

This happens all too often.

People put their yes on the table only to retract it when the going gets tough, or the feelings start to fade.

\* \* \*

**CONFORMITY**

Conformity is probably the most common result of those who hit the Dip. Conformity is all about succumbing to apathy. A person may stick with the relationship, but he or she no longer puts any effort into it.

Conformity leads to an existence without purpose and substance.

It's what Jesus condemns as being lukewarm to the Laodicean church in Revelation 3:15-16. Jesus tells the church that he will spit them out of his mouth because it's detestable. These aren't exactly the words you want to be have written to your church from Jesus himself!

In regards to a relationship with Christ, conformists are those who say they're Christians, but whose lives look identical to the rest of the world.

There is essentially no relationship. It's merely a title.

Conformists may or may not come to church, spend little or no time in prayer, sporadically read the Bible, rarely give, barely serve, and show little to no emotion when they either sing or talk about Jesus, yet still claim to have a relationship with Christ.

I'm pretty sure if I treated my wife the way most Christian conformists treat Christ, she might seriously think about quitting our marriage!

Apathetic conformists are like people who play sports, but only for fun. They don't care what happens. They're in the game, but not really playing to win. They have zero concern for the outcome.

Somewhere along the way, life eroded their soul, and they've forgotten their original promises. Because of this, selfishness and disregard for others seem to mark their lives.

* * *

### PERSEVERANCE

Rather than playing just for fun, Jesus calls us to play to win. This mentality is called perseverance. Peter exemplified perseverance when he stuck with Jesus after he called him back to fishing for men. From that point forward, Peter persevered for Christ. We know this because much of Peter's life is laid out for us in the Gospels and in the book of Acts.

Peter remained loyal to Jesus up to the very end when he was actually executed for his faith in Jesus. He never gave up.

Jesus' earthly brother had these words to say about perseverance in James 1:2-4:

> *Consider it pure joy, my brothers, when you face trials of many kinds, because you know that the testing of your faith develops perseverance. Perseverance must finish its work so that you may be mature and complete, not lacking in anything...*

Perseverance is vital because the reality is that life's not easy.

Make no mistake about it: trials will come our direction.

Remember, Jesus himself warned us of this truth when he said there would be many troubles in this life. Nonetheless, our perspective through the trials is what helps us endure through difficult circumstances.

Perseverance also has a purpose.

This is such an important concept to burn into our brains as we realign our perspectives.

God desires for us to be like Jesus.

Consider 1 John 2:6 that states,
"*Whoever claims to walk in him must walk as Jesus did.*"

In the passage quoted from James on the previous page, this Christ-likeness is referred to as being complete and mature. In order for us to reach this place in our own lives, and become the people God desires us to be, we must go through testing.

For as the apostle Paul said to the Roman Christians,

"*Not only so, but we also rejoice in our sufferings, because we know that suffering produces perseverance; perseverance, character; and character, hope. And hope does not disappoint us, because God has poured out his love into our hearts by the Holy Spirit, whom he has been given us.*" (Romans 5:3-5)

What exactly does it mean to persevere?

Perseverance means...
    ...clinging to Jesus no matter what.
    ...not giving up.
    ...enduring through difficult times knowing that the best is yet to come.
    ...knowing a day will come when feelings again surge, and remaining faithful in the period of waiting.
    ...not letting others shape us, but letting Christ do the shaping.
    ...trusting that what Jesus says is true, and that he holds true to his Word.
    ...standing on Jesus' promise that he will not leave us or forsake us.
    ...believing Jesus is on our side, and he always provides the best for us

In Romans 8:31-39, Paul beautifully and eloquently proclaims the hope in perseverance:

> *What, then, shall we say in response to this? If God is for us, who can be against us? He who did not spare his own Son, but gave him up for us all—how will he not also, along with him, graciously give us all things? Who will bring any charge against those whom God has chosen? It is God who justifies. Who is he that condemns? Christ Jesus who died—more than that, who was raised to life—is at the right hand of God and is also interceding for us. Who shall separate us from the love of Christ? Shall trouble or hardship or persecution or famine or nakedness or danger or sword? As it is written:*
>
> *"For your sake we face death all day long; we are considered as sheep to be slaughtered." No, in all these things we are more than conquerors through him who loved us. For I am convinced that neither death nor life, neither angels nor demons, neither the present nor the future, nor any powers, neither height nor depth, nor anything else in all creation, will be able to separate us from the love of God that is in Christ Jesus our Lord.*

When we have this confidence and security, we realize that Jesus is worth it, despite what we may or may not be feeling. The realistic ebb and flow of life takes us through many ups and downs, but we must resolve to keep looking up, no matter what. There are mountaintops and valleys, but the greatest soil is always found in the valleys! Perhaps this is why Jesus calls us both to be good soil, as well as to persevere. The two go hand-in-hand.

The declaration of perseverance is simply this:
*This relationship is worth my full commitment.*

When Peter came to terms with this truth, he responded to Jesus' call and found fulfillment. Jesus' pursuing grace beckoned him back and pulled him out of the Dip. It must be noted, though, that just because Peter got pulled out of the Dip, this isn't to say Peter never Dipped again.

The Dip is certain to come and go in every relationship throughout the course of a lifetime. Because of his commitment, though, Peter had the proper perspective when the next Dip hit.

Additionally, it's important to note that perseverance is not the same thing as perfection. Just because Peter gained the proper perspective, and realized that he would have to be a man of perseverance, doesn't mean he was perfect from that point forward. He still struggled throughout his days and had to continue coming to Jesus for forgiveness and hope.

Around a year and a half later, Peter would blatantly deny Jesus three times, as seen in John 18:15-18, 25-27. Jesus even questioned his love three times after his resurrection in John 21. Peter was far from perfect, but he learned to persevere in pursuit of perfection.

When all is said and done, perseverance is about remembering the lavish, undeserving grace of Jesus over and over again. For when such grace grabs at our hearts, we realize that nothing else on the entire planet is worth pursuing.

The grace of Christ meets us where we're at, and takes us to a place we could never get to on our own.

Alone, Peter caught nothing.
With Christ, there were more fish than the nets could hold.

If only we really believed this truth about Jesus, it would change everything we've ever known, and bring us through every Dip we could ever encounter.

Jesus' grace is enough.
He hasn't quit on you.
He's so rich in love.

* * *

[ CHAPTER FOUR // 63 ]

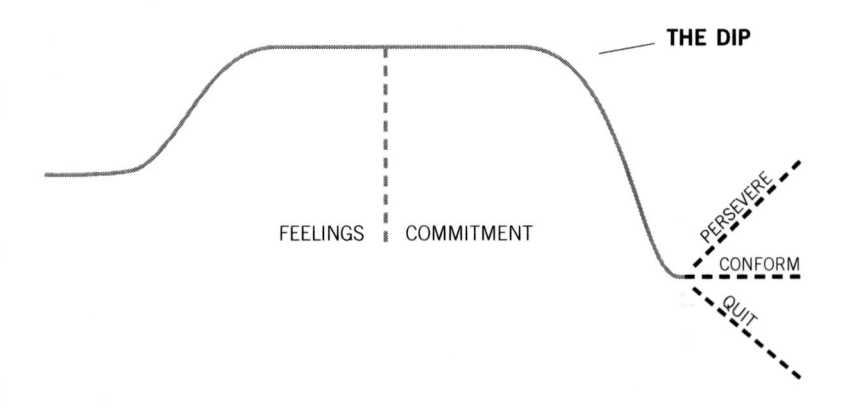

```
                    ___ THE DIP

         FEELINGS | COMMITMENT    PERSEVERE
                                   CONFORM
                                    QUIT
```

***Are you someone that perseveres, conforms, or have you already quit?***

May the grace of Jesus bring you to your knees and reassure you not to be afraid.

And if you need any further proof of his love, look no further than the cross…

# [ CHAPTER FIVE ]
# You Lead, and I'll Follow

*"You lead, and I'll follow."*

From the beginning of our marriage, Jamie and I have wanted our relationship to glorify Jesus.

We said from the start that we don't want to be a couple that starts off in the right direction, but ends up at the wrong destination. We didn't want to start by pursuing and trusting Jesus, only to eventually get sidetracked, and end up looking like everyone else that doesn't live for Jesus.

Through our marriage, we really wanted people to get an accurate picture of Jesus' love for the church as expressed in Ephesians 5:21-33. In order for this to be the case, my wife has made it clear that I must lead her well. She reminds me of this simply by saying, *"You lead, and I'll follow."*

If I lead in initiating Bible studies and prayer, she'll follow me.
If I lead in living sacrificially, she'll follow me.
If I lead in taking steps of faith and trusting Jesus more, she'll follow me.

If I desire our marriage to glorify Jesus, I must lead and she'll follow me.

Don't mistake Jamie's role of following as a lesser role, or think this means her faith is not her own. Don't think that my wife only serves Jesus because I serve Jesus. That's hardly the case. My wife has walked much longer with Christ than I have, and she inspires me in my faith daily. But the reason my wife encourages me to lead is because this is the pattern Scripture lays out for an integrity-filled marriage.

Integrity is never asking anyone to do anything that you first haven't done.

Integrity is being the pacesetter.

Integrity is proving you are trustworthy and worth following because you lead the way.

Simply, you walk the walk and don't just talk the talk.

Therefore, when I ask my wife and our family to go after Jesus with their whole hearts, I better be going after Jesus with my whole heart, too! If I'm not, I lack integrity. It's just lip service.

**Will you follow if Jesus is leading the way?**

\* \* \*

*It was just before the Passover Feast. Jesus knew that the time had come for him to leave this world and go to the Father. Having loved his own who were in the world, he now showed them the full extent of his love. The evening meal was being served, and the devil had already prompted Judas Iscariot, the son of Simon, to betray Jesus. Jesus knew that the Father had put all things under his power, and that he had come from God and was returning to God; so he got up from the meal, took off his outer clothing, and wrapped a towel around his waist. After that, he poured water into a basin and began to wash his disciples' feet, drying them with the towel that was wrapped around him.*

*He came to Simon Peter, who said to him, "Lord, are you going to wash my feet?" Jesus replied, "You do not realize now what I am doing, but later you will understand." "No," said Peter, "you shall never wash my feet." Jesus answered, "Unless I wash you, you have no part with me." "Then, Lord," Simon Peter replied, "not just my feet but my hands and my head as well!" Jesus answered, "A person who has had a bath needs only to wash his feet; his whole body is clean. And you are clean, though not every one of you." For he knew who was going to betray him, and that was why he said not every one was clean.*

*When he had finished washing their feet, he put on his clothes and returned to his place. "Do you understand what I have done for you?" he asked them. "You call me 'Teacher' and 'Lord,' and rightly so, for that is what I am. Now that I, your Lord and Teacher, have washed your feet, you also should wash one another's feet. I have set you an example that you should do as I have done for you. I tell you the truth, no servant is greater than his master, nor is a messenger greater than the one who sent him. Now that you know these things, you will be blessed if you do them.*
*-John 13:1-17*

Fast forward about a year and a half after we last saw Peter on his knees at the feet of Jesus, and what we find is a complete role reversal.

Jesus is now on his knees at the feet of Peter.

It was the evening before Roman soldiers took Jesus to be put on trial for his actions and eventually crucified. It was the last meal Jesus would have with his disciples. Jesus was fully aware of what fate had in store for him. With mere hours left to live, he chose to spend his time with the men he'd been teaching and traveling with over the past three years.

I believe this is a decision many of us would make, too. We would desire to spend time with those we cherish if we knew our time was coming to an end. Such a decision makes sense. However, the way Jesus chooses to spend those final hours astonishes me.

The evening meal had been served, and after eating, Jesus got up, wrapped a towel around his waist, poured water into a basin, and began washing the feet of his disciples, and drying them with the towel. Would this be how you would choose to spend your last night with your band of brothers?

Such a spectacle would have been shocking and embarrassing for the disciples to witness.

Jewish rabbis and sages of the day said the only people allowed to wash feet were Gentile slaves. Hebrew slaves were not even allowed to wash feet, because it was considered degrading even to them. The Mishnah, a collection of ancient rabbi interpretations, states,

> "All manner of service that a slave must render to his master a student must render to his teacher, except that of taking off his shoe. A Hebrew slave must not wash the feet of his master, nor put his shoes on him."

In this time, there were no shoes to cover one's feet to keep them clean. Additionally, there were few paved roads, and the only form of transportation was on animals.

Thus, feet were most definitely covered in dust and dung.
People's feet were filthy.

This was a primary reason that foot washing was scorned. This gesture was appalling to Peter as he exclaims in verse 8, *"No, you should never wash my feet."* Peter couldn't fathom Jesus now being at his feet performing such a degrading act.

This then begs the question: *Why would he do it?*

The author, John, answers this question in verse 13 when Jesus says, *"I have set you an example that you should do as I have done for you."* Earlier in verse 1 John writes that Jesus did this to *"show them the full extent of his love."*

I would summarize these two verses by claiming Jesus washed the feet of the disciples to model integrity, as well as the reality of true love.

Throughout this book, the life of Peter has been the primary scriptural focus. I believe that in his life we see an accurate reflection of many of our lives.

You could say that Peter's story is many of our stories.

His relationship with Jesus consists of ups and downs, highs and lows, following and fishing. Peter is someone who yearns to follow Jesus, but at times struggles because he hits the Dip. In the last chapter, we discovered how perseverance was Jesus' call for Peter when he hit the dreaded Dip, and we saw how the element of trust heightened his ability to persevere.

The same is true for us.

Do we really trust the promises of Jesus to the point that we actually stick with him, no matter what?

Do we believe Jesus is worth our perseverance?

I believe this question lingered in Peter's mind, because he is the disciple the author primarily highlights as Jesus washes the disciples' feet. In this moment, Jesus was choosing to build Peter's trust in leading by example. For when we first do what we are asking others to do, integrity is displayed, which ultimately cultivates trust.

This is why in verse 13, Jesus tells Peter he's setting an example for him and the rest of the gang to follow. To set an example means that Jesus is going first.

He's setting the pace.
He's leading and paving the way.
He's not asking them to do anything he first hasn't done.

This is the essence of integrity and in doing so, Jesus is building trust and credibility in Peter's heart to help him persevere. Seeing Jesus on his knees before him gave Peter a tangible portrayal of the trustworthiness of Jesus, because he was willing to do that which was difficult and undesired.

Jesus was willing to serve.

This is the reality of true love.

*Love is* a call to lead by example in serving others.
*Love is* a call to serve even when it doesn't feel good.
*Love is* a call to move forward even when others might chastise your actions.
*Love is* a call to count others more significant than yourself.
*Love is* a call to take the lowest position so that we can lift others up.
*Love is* a call to humble ourselves so others can receive dignity.

How different would our relationships look if this were the perspective and posture from which we acted?

We desperately want the feeling of love, but do we want the reality of the love Jesus is exemplifying here?

For when we're willing to wash the feet of others, we look like Jesus.

Would you not be willing to persevere for someone that was willing to do what Jesus did here?

In just a few hours, Jesus would trump this event when he stretched out his arms to be crucified for all mankind. Such an undeserving sacrifice proves his love for all of us. It proves he's worth giving our lives to because he gave his life for us.

Once again, this is integrity.

Jesus told Peter in Matthew 16:24 that if anyone wanted to come after him, he must deny himself, take up his cross, and follow. When Jesus said this to Peter, it was probably shocking, and possibly seemed extreme, until Jesus displayed this truth by literally denying himself, taking up his cross, and following the plan of his Heavenly Father.

Can you imagine how much more inclined Peter was to take up his cross and follow Jesus after witnessing Jesus' integrity in practicing what he preached?

Jesus never asks us to do anything that he has not already done first himself.

This fosters trust…
 …dependence.
 …transparency.
 …empathy.
 …concern.
 …genuineness.
 …relationship.
 …true, committed love.
 …perseverance.

Additionally, we know that we can trust the words of Jesus to persevere throughout the Dip because in Jesus' last days we see that he experienced the Dip, too.

A few short hours after the Passover meal, Jesus went to the Garden of Gethsemane to pray. The words of Jesus' prayer recorded in Luke 22:42 are startling:

*"Father, if you are willing, take this cup from me; yet not my will, but yours be done."*

In this moment, Jesus is asking the Father to reconsider his plan.

He's pleading for another way. He knows that what's in store is going to be humiliating and painful. It would be easy for Jesus to throw in the towel in this moment and quite honestly, who would blame him?

However, praise God Jesus didn't quit! He persevered proclaiming not his will, but God's will be done. Jesus stuck with the relationship even when the feelings weren't warm and fuzzy.

We can do likewise.

But this isn't the only episode of Jesus hitting the Dip.

In Matthew 27:46, Jesus was on the cross of Calvary carrying the weight of the world's sins, including your sins and mine, and he cried out to the Father,

*"My God, my God, why have you forsaken me?"*

The cross screams the Dip.

This was when all feelings had faded, and commitment had to fully kick in.
This is when all hope seemed gone.
This was the loneliest and most painful moment for Jesus.

Take comfort and know that you're not alone in your Dip.
Jesus trekked the Dip before you or I ever took a single breath.
His integrity demanded it.

But while the cross screams the Dip, the empty tomb screams perseverance and true love. For Jesus' perseverance brought forth the possibility of hope for all mankind. Death could not hold down the Son of God.

Three days after his crucifixion—three days after it appeared the Dip had gotten the best of Jesus—he burst forth from the grave. Jesus was fully alive and now fully offering hope to all who put their faith in his death on the cross as the just payment for their sins.

Jesus conquered the grave. Jesus also conquered the Dip.

But it's vitally important that we listen to the words Jesus spoke to his disciples after he finished washing their feet. These words from John 13:17 contain within them the ultimate truth of all relationships:

> *"Now that you know these things, you will be blessed if you do them."*

It's one thing to know about Jesus' call to persevere through the Dip.
*It's completely another thing to do it.*

It's one thing to look at Jesus' integrity and trust that he's worth following.
*It's completely another thing to actually follow him.*

The reality is that going back to fishing is always easier than following. You need look no further than Peter to prove this. But what we must take away more than anything else from the life of Peter is that he possessed integrity as well.

When he heard the word, *he acted.*
When he realized he was wrong, *he changed.*
When he realized he wasn't fully committed, *he committed.*
When he realized he didn't fully trust in the promises of Christ, *he trusted.*
When Jesus set an example for him to follow, *he followed.*

So it must be with us, too.

I once heard in a sermon that the measuring stick of our lives is the distance between when we hear something we know God wants us to do and the time it takes for us to actually do it.

I couldn't agree more.

And when we act on what we know, Jesus promises that we will be blessed. The blessing is his presence, provision, and protection in our lives.
I don't know about you, but I want the blessing of God in my life.

The way to have it is simply to do what Jesus led the way in doing.

Jesus led.

*Will you follow?*

# [ EPILOGUE ]
# Living So Others Ask Why

*"I just want to live in a way so that others ask why."*

By this point in the book, you've likely figured out that every chapter has started with a quote from my wife, whom I love dearly. I try my best to pay close attention to what she says because she always has great and inspiring things to say.

The quote above seems like a fitting way to end this book. We were sitting at Starbucks at one of our Friday morning coffee shop Bible-study dates, reading through Hebrews 12 when we landed on verse 14. It reads,

> *"Make every effort to live in peace with all men and to be holy; without holiness no one will see the Lord."*

After reading that verse, we didn't get any further because we began discussing how to live holy lives. We talked about how heavy our hearts were because of the many people we both knew that started the journey with Jesus, but whom the Dip got the best of. We pondered what it would take to help people tangibly see the goodness of God and deem Him worthy of following, no matter what.

It was then that my wife said,
"*I just want to live in a way so that others ask why.*"

Immediately, I clung to the phrase. This is how we must live if we want people to see God, and if we want to inspire them to persevere. And when people do ask why, we'll point to Jesus.

Why...
- ... do you stick with it when things are difficult?
- ... do you not give up on each other?
- ... do you not get stressed and worried when things go wrong in your life?
- ... do you love people that don't love you back?
- ... are you content with what you have and not always wanting more?
- ... do you still believe in the church?
- ... do you not care what others think about you?
- ... do you listen to people's problems?
- ... do you believe people can change?

I really believe this is what it's going to take for people to see that a relationship with Christ is worth pursuing and persevering for to the very end.

People must tangibly see Jesus through our lives.

This means we need to trust what Jesus calls us to and actually do it. Those of us that follow Christ are to be the proof of God to a watching, desperate, broken, hungry, consumeristic, and lonely world.

Our lives must declare that Jesus is worthy of our commitment.

And we can do these things, because we've discovered that Jesus has already paved the way. He is the personification of integrity. We can trust the way he calls us to live because he lived that very life.

In Jesus, we see a life put on full display that shows us why committing to a relationship with God is worthwhile.

Simply stated, Jesus lived in such a way that caused us to ask why.

I believe this only happens if we all determine to find ourselves in the same position Peter was in after he saw the huge haul of fish—on our knees before Jesus, completely trusting in His goodness. This would catalyze us to actually live out the promises Jesus makes in the Bible, because in this position we see His infinite grace and continual calling.

Was this not the case for Peter?

Although he encountered the Dip, Jesus didn't give up on him! His ability to be used by Christ was not stolen away because of a few rough patches. Jesus offered grace and continued calling Peter to live in such a way that caused others to ask why. And Peter responded.

In the first part of the book of Acts, we find Peter emerging as the focal leader of the Church. In Acts 1, Jesus has recently risen from the dead, commissioned them to go and make disciples, and ascended into heaven.

In Acts 2, Peter proclaims to a large crowd their need to repent and be baptized in the name of Jesus because the resurrection has proven beyond a shadow of a doubt that Jesus is the one. Acts 2:41 tells us that about three thousand were added to their number that day.
(Not bad for your first sermon!)

In Acts 3, Peter heals a crippled beggar in the name of Jesus. This astonishes the onlookers. Peter proceeds to tell the astonished people this miracle came from the power of Jesus working through him.

In Acts 4, Jewish authorities are angered over this healing because they don't want people putting their trust in Jesus. This moment has potential to become a people Dip for Peter. Not this time, though. Peter boldly declares that Jesus is the source of healing, and that *"salvation is found in no one else, for there is no other name under heaven given to men by which we must be saved" (Acts 4:12).*

Verse 13 then reads,

> "When they saw the courage of Peter and John and realized that they were unschooled, ordinary men, they were astonished and they took note that these men had been with Jesus."

They noticed Peter and others were living differently, and this caused them to ask why. And when they asked why, Peter didn't hesitate to speak the name of Jesus. This must be true of you and I, too.

We must live in a way so that people recognize that we're ordinary people that have been with Jesus. This comes through our willingness to follow and obey everything he says.

This is what causes others to ask why.

Peter did this all the way up to the point of his death.
Once he had encountered the grace of Jesus, he knew Jesus was worth persevering for, even to the point of death.

Ancient church history records that Peter's life ended on a cross just like Jesus. He too was crucified because he never stopped testifying to the goodness of Christ. The only exception was that Peter's crucifixion was upside down because he didn't deem himself worthy to die in the exact same manner as his Lord and Savior.

I have to believe such an act caused onlookers to ask why.

What about us?
What will our story be?

I love Peter's story, because I believe that in it we find our story.

If that's the case, are we willing to persevere and cause others to ask why just like Peter?

When the Dip hits, will we still cling to the grace and calling of Jesus?

A lot of people quit.
Quitting is easy.

Even more conform.
Like chameleons, they blend in with everyone else around them and live the same life everyone else lives.

Quitting and conforming will never provoke the question of why.

Perseverance will, though.

Rocks and thorns may have defined the soil of your life in the past, but it doesn't have to stay that way. Never forget that each year the ground changes based upon the weather conditions.

Rocks and thorns one year can quickly become fertile, good soil the next. May the same be true in the soil of our hearts when the Dip hits.

In a world of constant fickleness, break-ups, divorces, relativism, and so much negativity, perseverance will be the light that will shine forth in the dark world. It will prompt the question of why.

And when it does, we can introduce them to Jesus.

They'll honeymoon for a while and eventually plateau and maybe even hit the Dip. But if they have realistic expectations from the beginning, are determined to stick with it, and know that Jesus can be trusted, no matter what, their perseverance will make the light even brighter.

Without holiness no one will see God.
I believe that living holy is living so that others ask why.

I pray you persevere so others ask why and see our Lord.

I think it's fitting to end with some words from Peter's own lips in 1 Peter 1:8-9. May this be your motivation through the Dip and beyond into everlasting life...

> *"Though you have not seen him, you love him; and even though you do not see him now, you believe in him and are filled with an inexpressible and glorious joy, for you are receiving the goal of your faith, the salvation of your souls."*

* * *

[ EPILOGUE // 81 ]

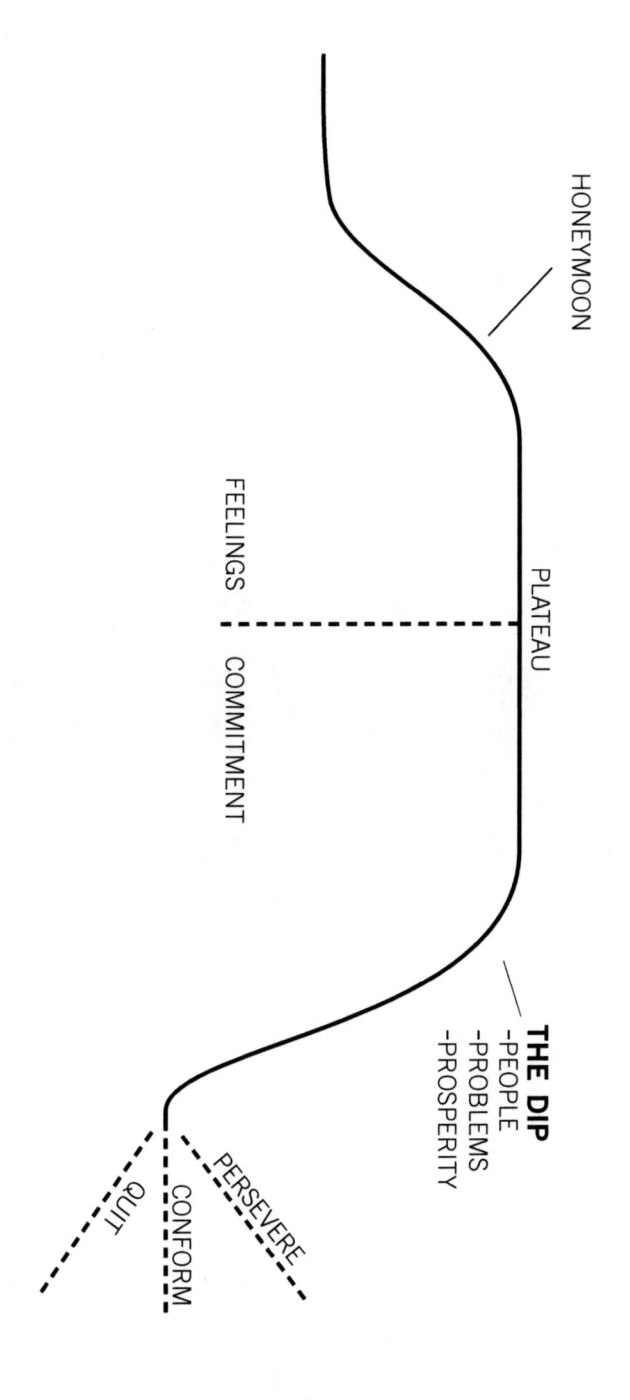

HONEYMOON

FEELINGS
———
COMMITMENT

PLATEAU

**THE DIP**
- PEOPLE
- PROBLEMS
- PROSPERITY

QUIT
CONFORM
PERSEVERE